# HYMNS *for*
## CLASSICAL GUITAR

Arrangements by John Hill

ISBN 978-1-61780-369-7

HAL•LEONARD®

Visit Hal Leonard Online at
**www.halleonard.com**

Contact us:
**Hal Leonard**
7777 West Bluemound Road
Milwaukee, WI 53213
Email: info@halleonard.com

In Europe, contact:
**Hal Leonard Europe Limited**
42 Wigmore Street
Marylebone, London, W1U 2RN
Email: info@halleonardeurope.com

In Australia, contact:
**Hal Leonard Australia Pty. Ltd.**
4 Lentara Court
Cheltenham, Victoria, 3192 Australia
Email: info@halleonard.com.au

# CONTENTS

4   Abide with Me

7   All Hail the Power of Jesus' Name

8   Amazing Grace

10   Be Thou My Vision

14   Christ the Lord Is Risen Today

11   Come, Thou Fount of Every Blessing

16   Crown Him with Many Crowns

18   Fairest Lord Jesus

22   Faith of Our Fathers

21   For the Beauty of the Earth

24   God of Grace and God of Glory

26   Holy, Holy, Holy

28   In the Garden

30   Joyful, Joyful, We Adore Thee

32   A Mighty Fortress Is Our God

34   My Faith Looks Up to Thee

36   Nearer, My God, to Thee

42   O Sacred Head, Now Wounded

44   O Worship the King

39   The Old Rugged Cross

46   Praise to the Lord, the Almighty

48   Rock of Ages

50   Savior, Like a Shepherd Lead Us

53   Take My Life and Let It Be

54   What a Friend We Have in Jesus

# Abide with Me

**Words by Henry F. Lyte**
**Music by William H. Monk**

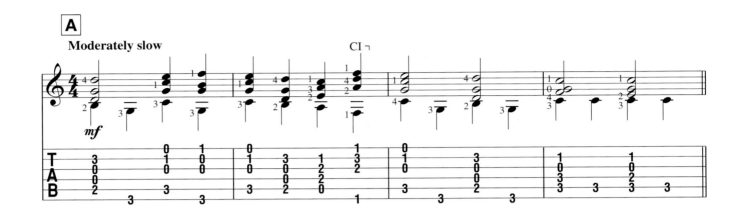

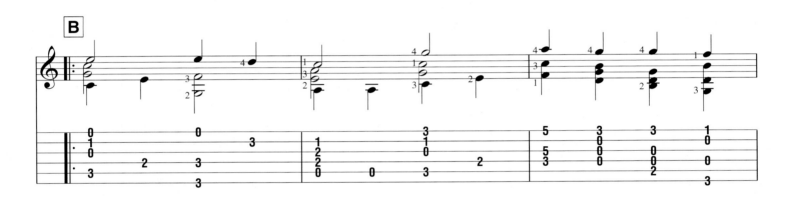

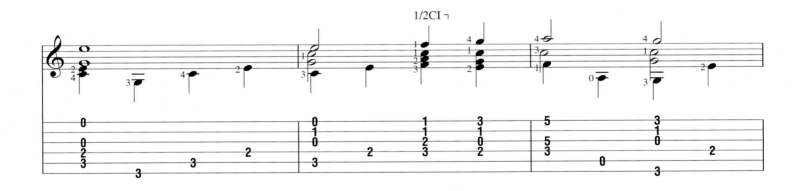

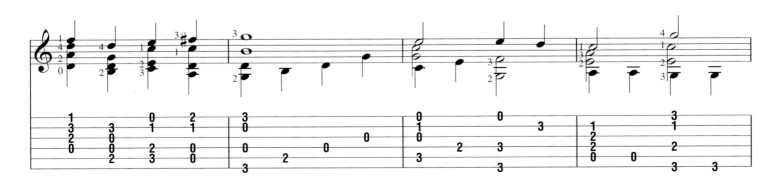

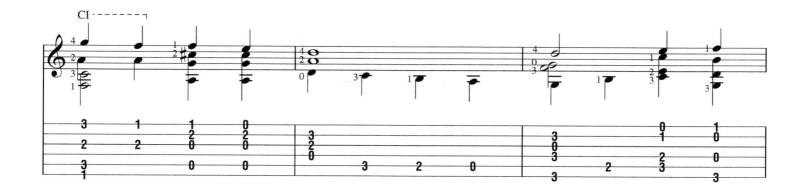

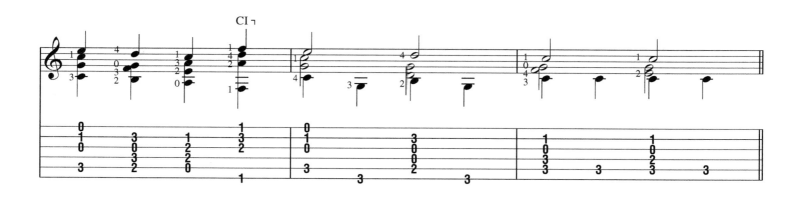

**C**

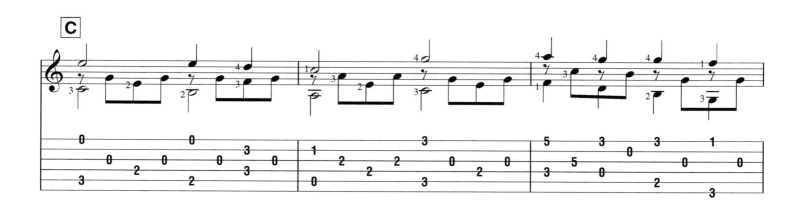

5

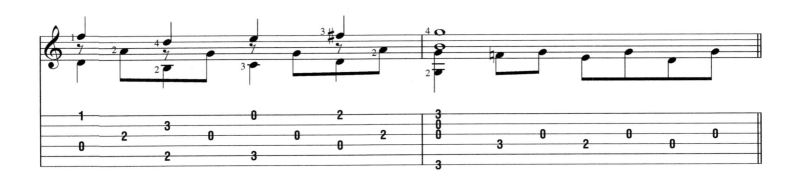

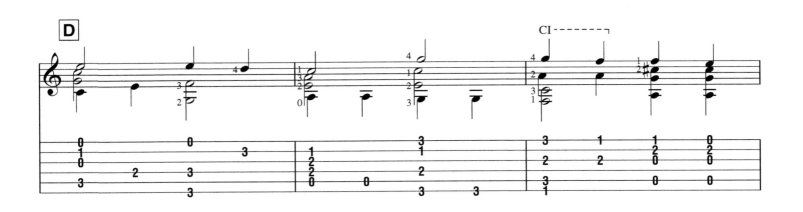

# All Hail the Power of Jesus' Name

**Words by Edward Perronet**
**Altered by John Rippon**
**Music by Oliver Holden**

# Amazing Grace

**Words by John Newton**
**From *A Collection of Sacred Ballads***
**Traditional American Melody**
**From Carrell and Clayton's *Virginia Harmony***
**Arranged by Edwin O. Excell**

Tuning:
(low to high) D-A-D-G-B-E

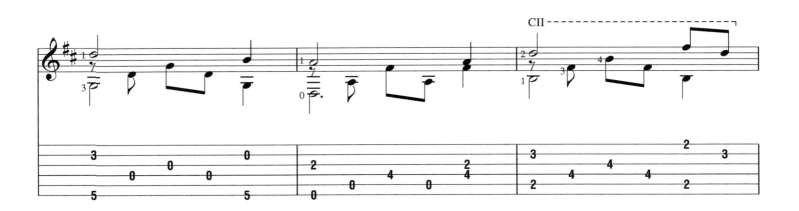

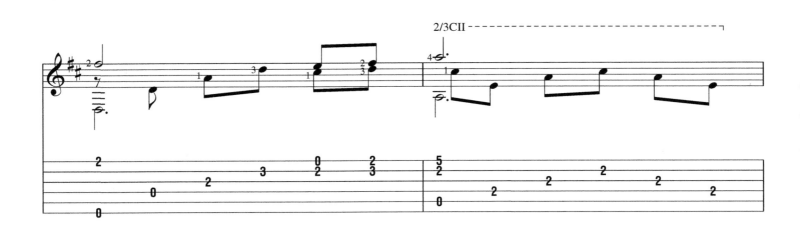

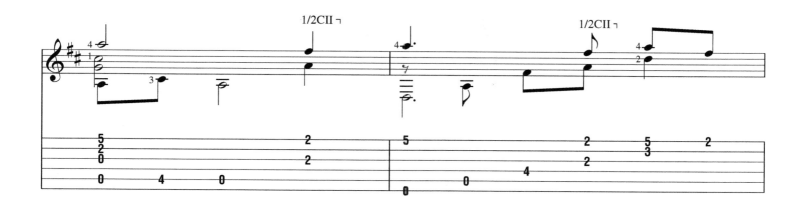

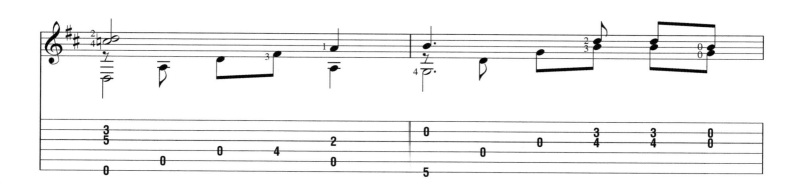

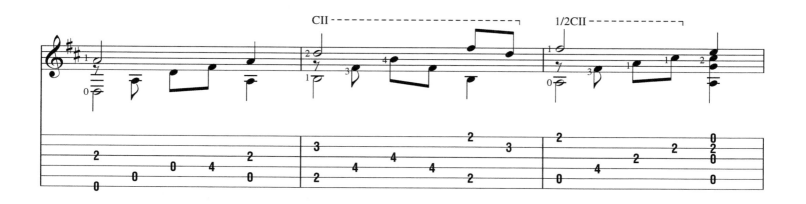

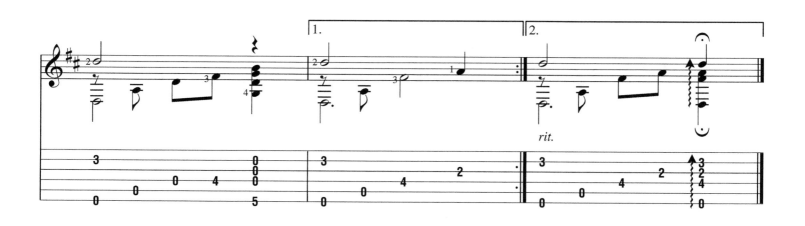

# Be Thou My Vision

Traditional Irish
Translated by Mary E. Byrne

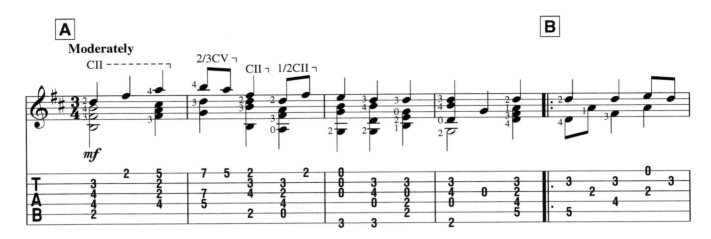

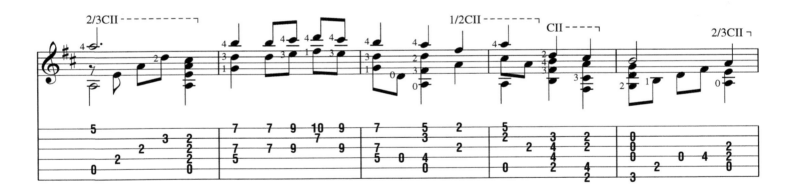

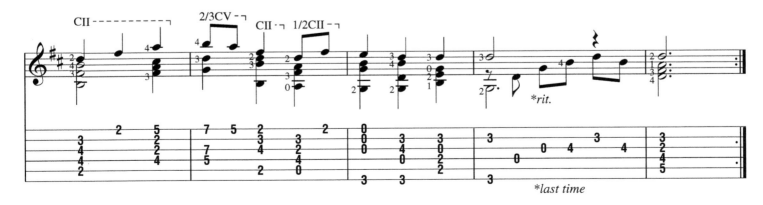

*last time

# Come, Thou Fount of Every Blessing

Words by Robert Robinson
Music from John Wyeth's *Repository of Sacred Music*

Tuning:
(low to high) D-A-D-G-B-E

# Christ the Lord Is Risen Today

**Words by Charles Wesley**
**Music adapted from *Lyra Davidica***

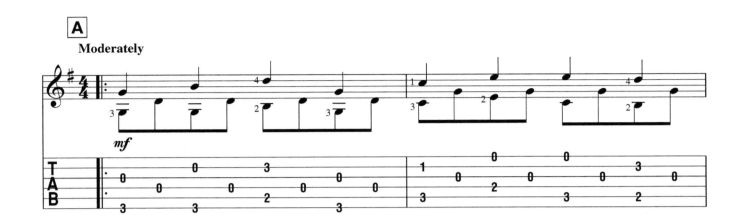

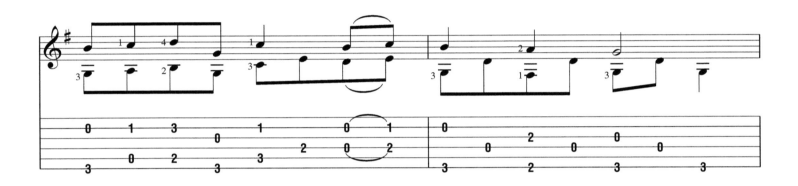

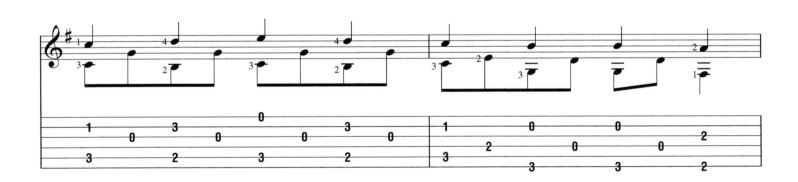

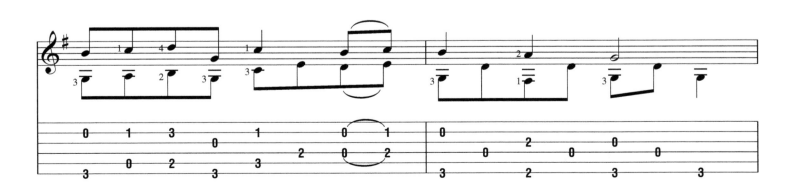

# Crown Him with Many Crowns

**Words by Matthew Bridges and Godfrey Thring**
**Music by George Job Elvey**

Tuning:
(low to high) D-A-D-G-B-E

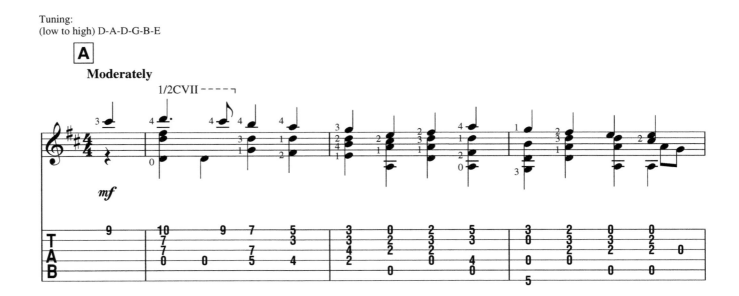

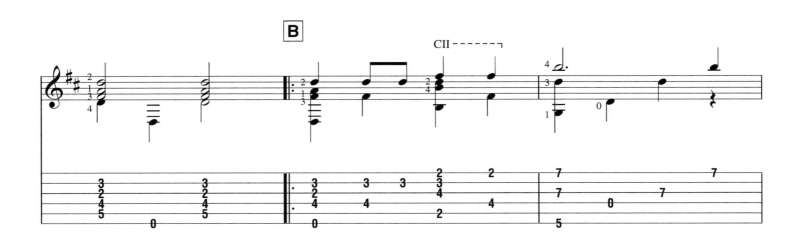

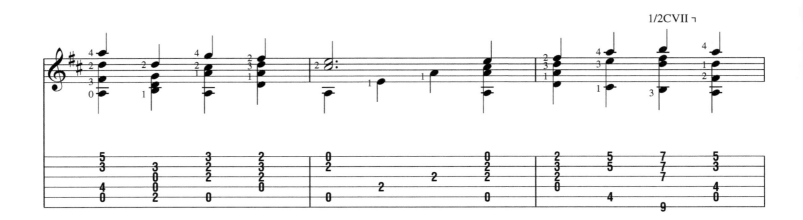

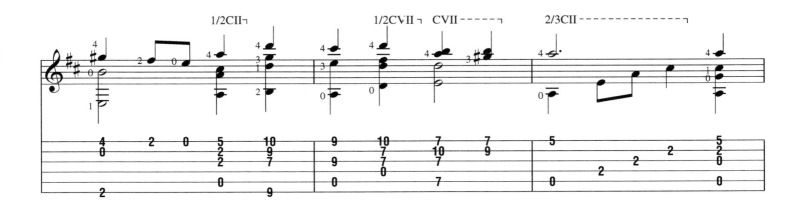

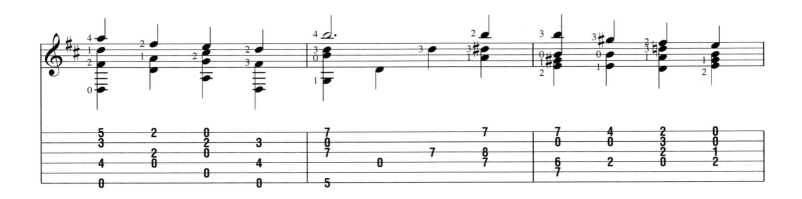

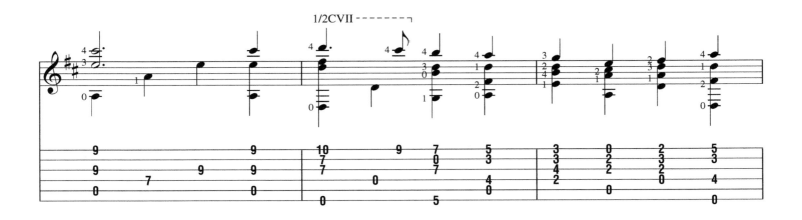

# Fairest Lord Jesus

**Words from *Munster Gesangbuch***
**Verse 4 by Joseph A. Seiss**
**Music from Schlesische Volkslieder**
**Arranged by Richard Storrs Willis**

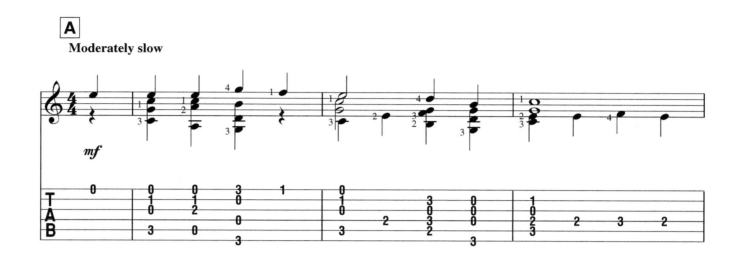

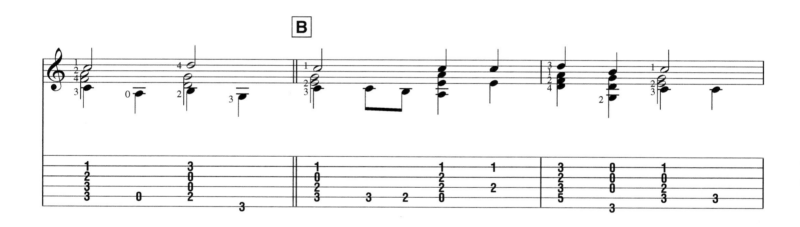

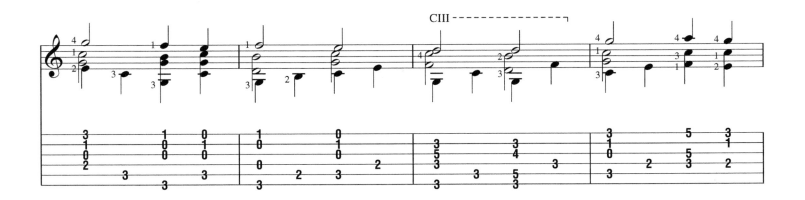

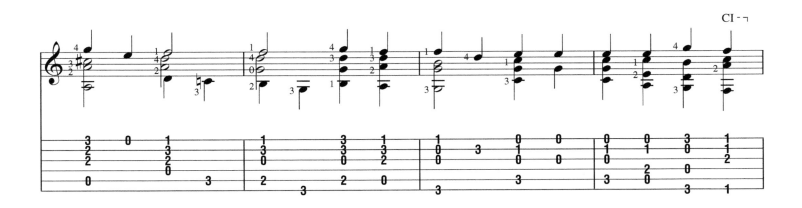

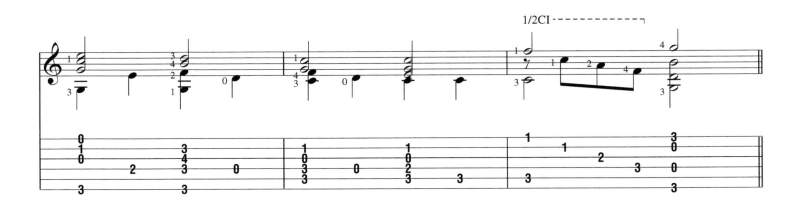

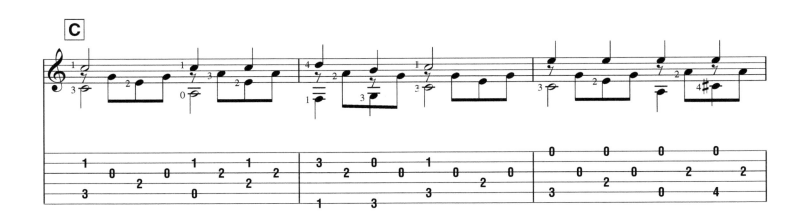

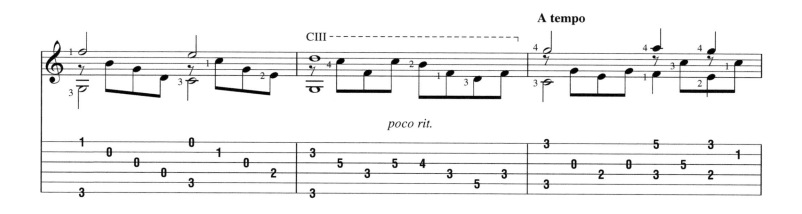

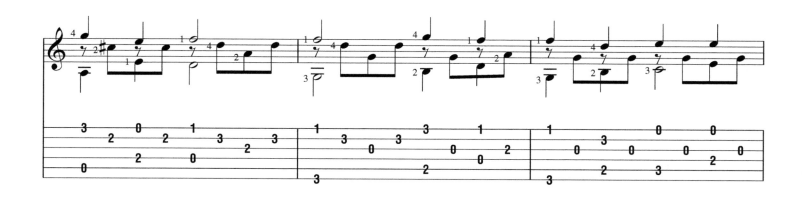

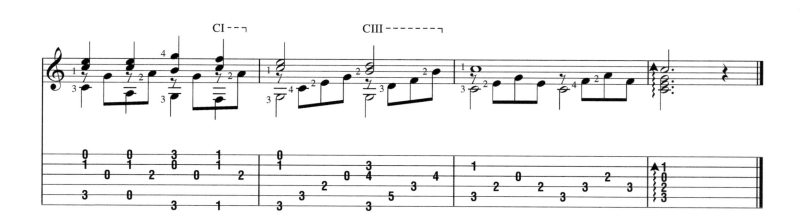

# For the Beauty of the Earth

**Words by Folliot S. Pierpoint**
**Music by Conrad Kocher**

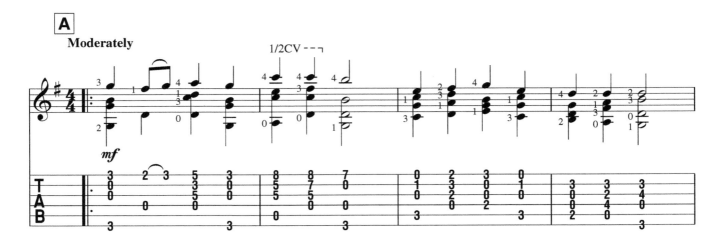

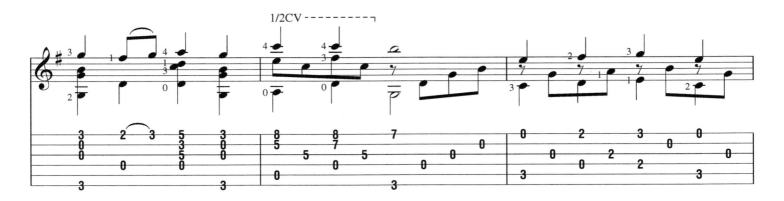

# Faith of Our Fathers

Words by Frederick William Faber
Music by Henri F. Hemy and James G. Walton

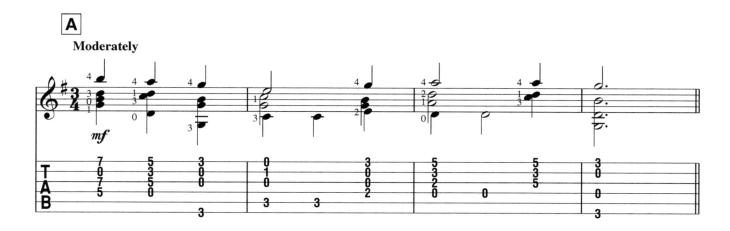

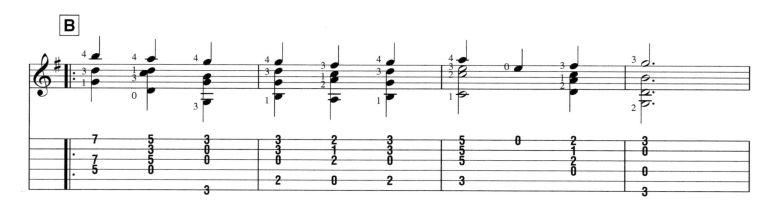

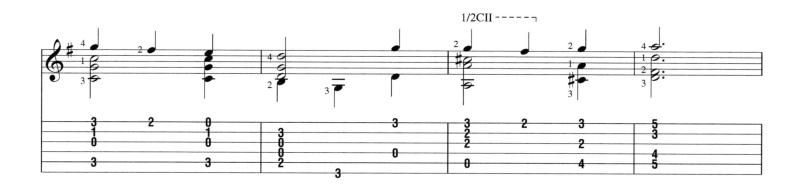

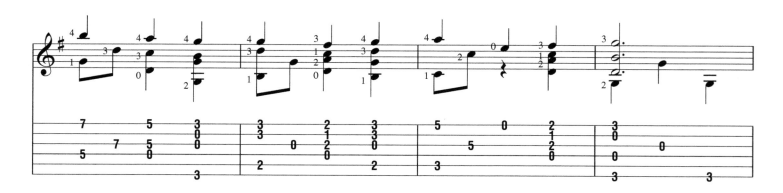

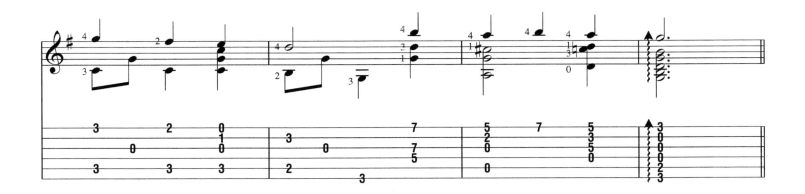

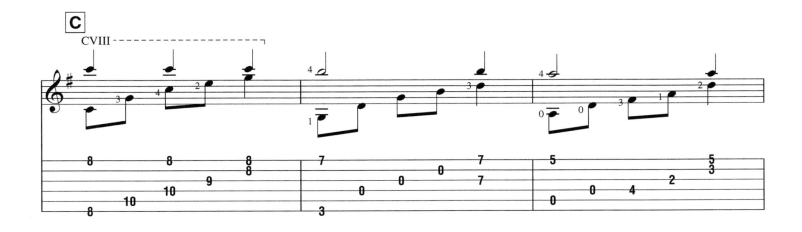

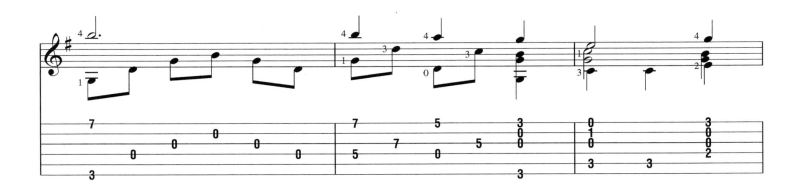

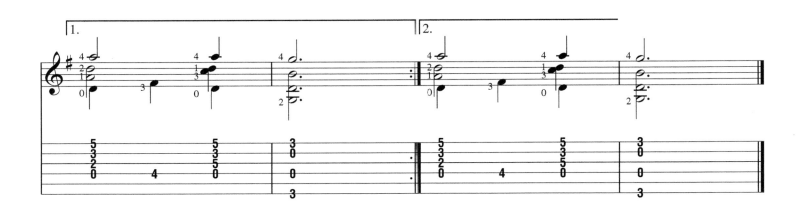

# God of Grace and God of Glory

**Words by Harry Emerson Fosdick**
**Music by John Hughes**

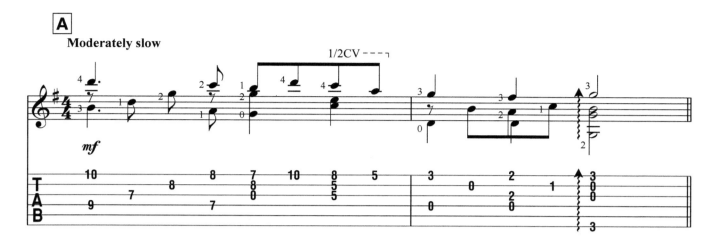

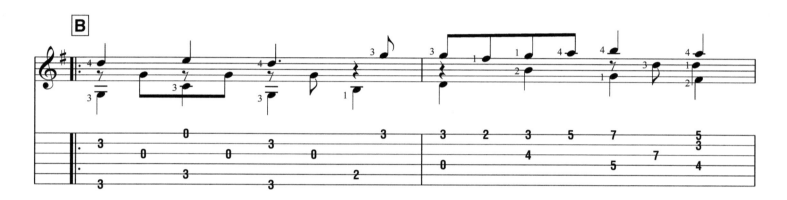

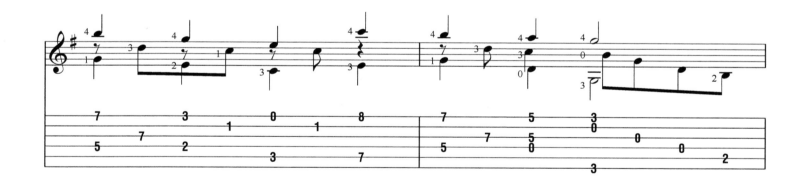

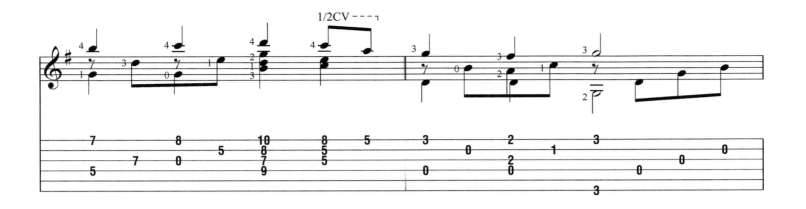

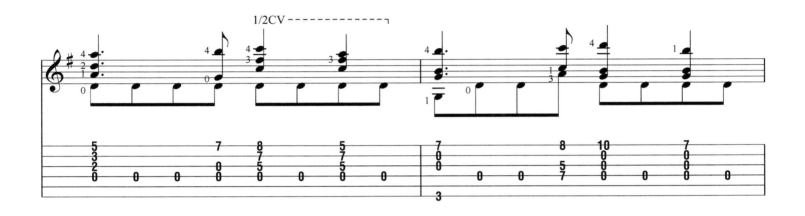

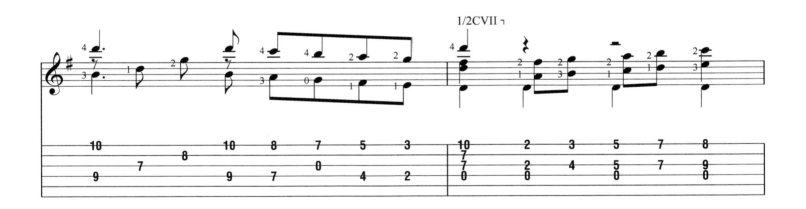

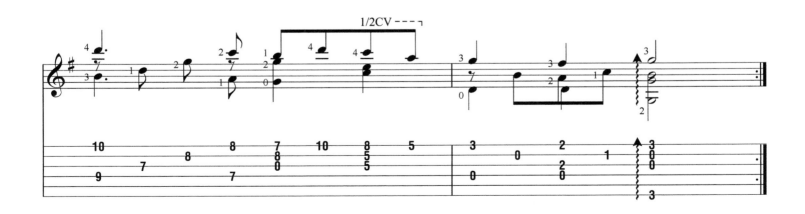

# Holy, Holy, Holy

Text by Reginald Heber
Music by John B. Dykes

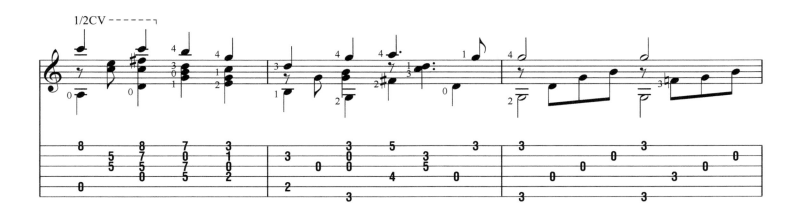

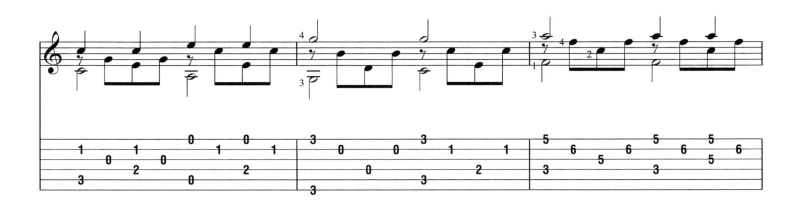

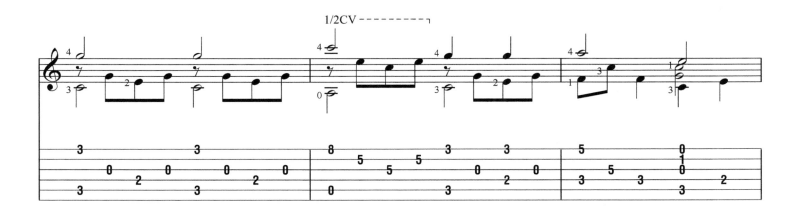

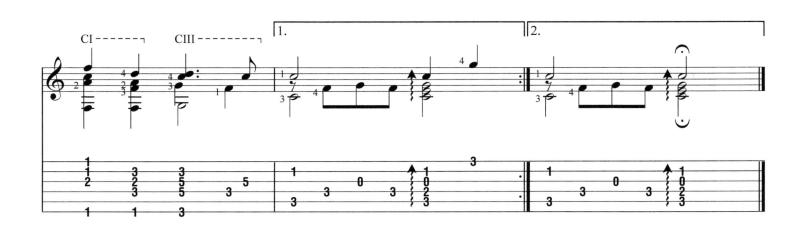

# In the Garden

**Words and Music by C. Austin Miles**

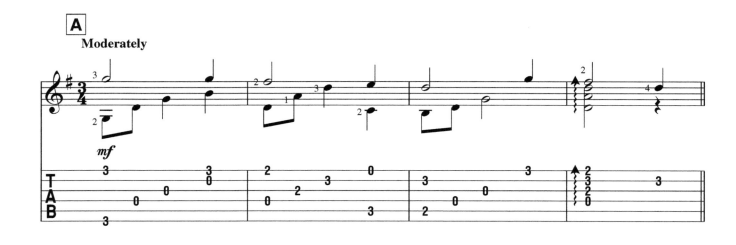

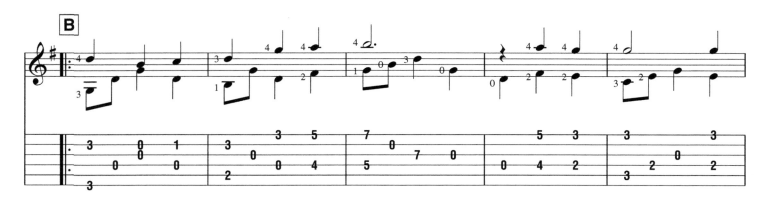

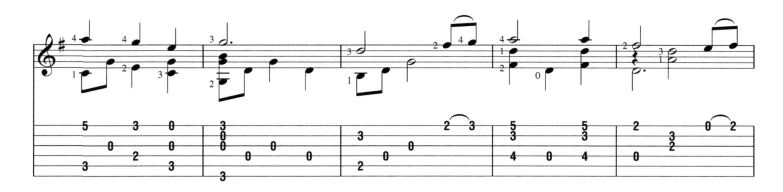

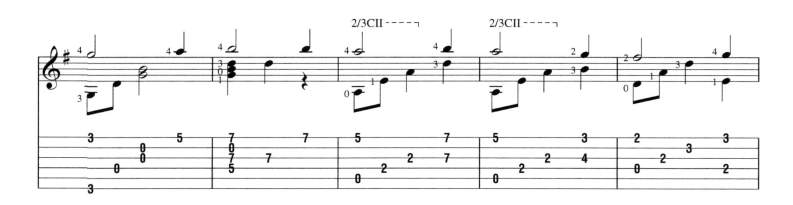

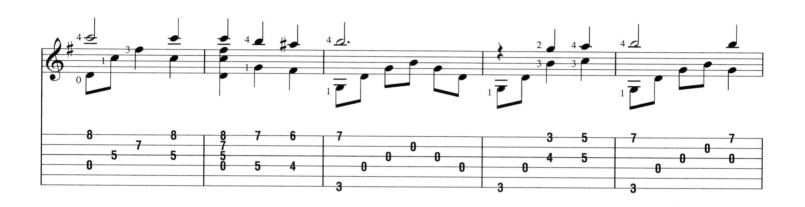

# Joyful, Joyful, We Adore Thee

**Words by Henry van Dyke**
**Music by Ludwig van Beethoven, melody from Ninth Symphony**
**Adapted by Edward Hodges**

Tuning:
(low to high) D-A-D-G-B-E

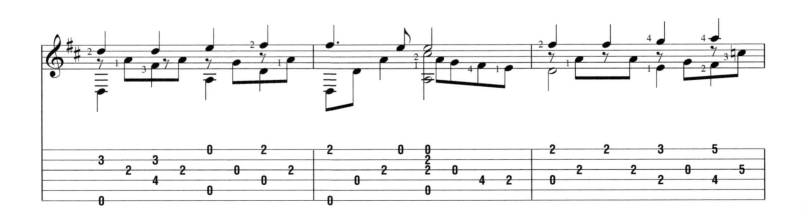

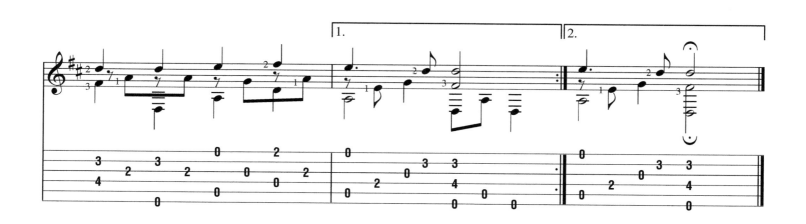

# A Mighty Fortress Is Our God

Words and Music by Martin Luther
Translated by Frederick H. Hedge
Based on Psalm 46

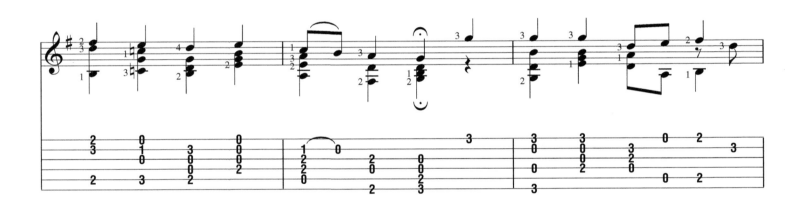

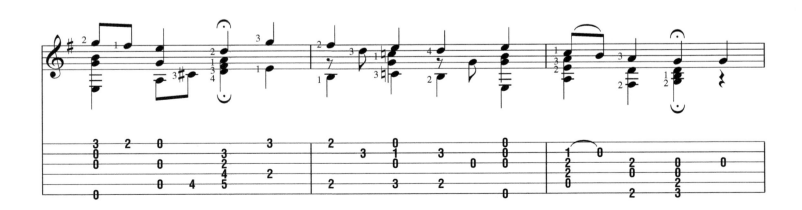

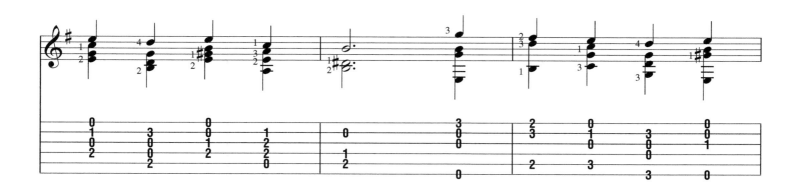

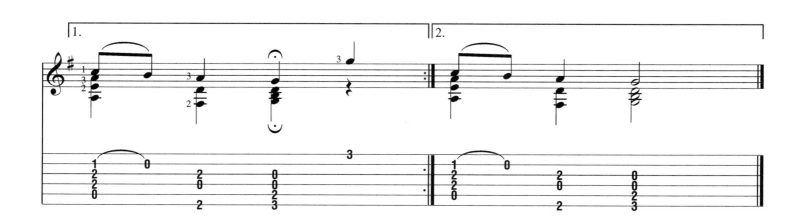

# My Faith Looks Up to Thee

**Words by Ray Palmer**
**Music by Lowell Mason**

Tuning:
(low to high) D-A-D-G-B-E

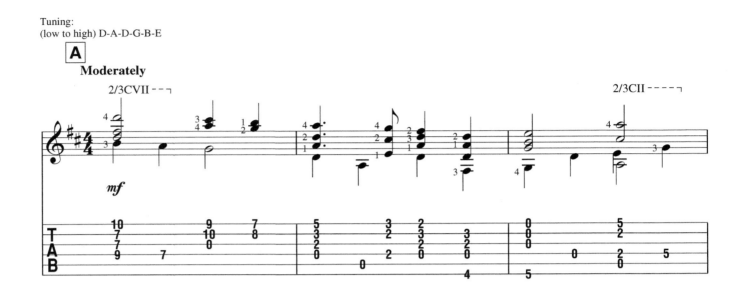

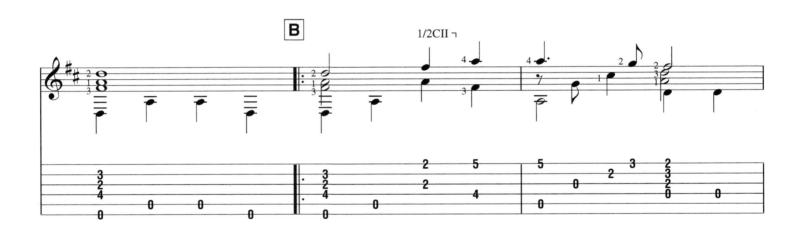

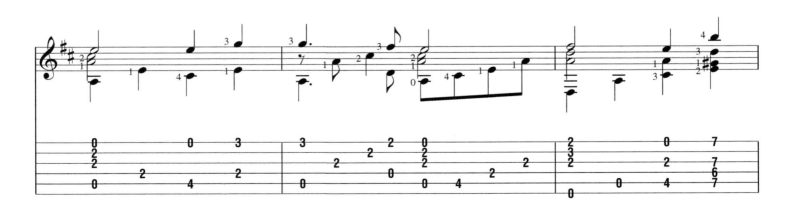

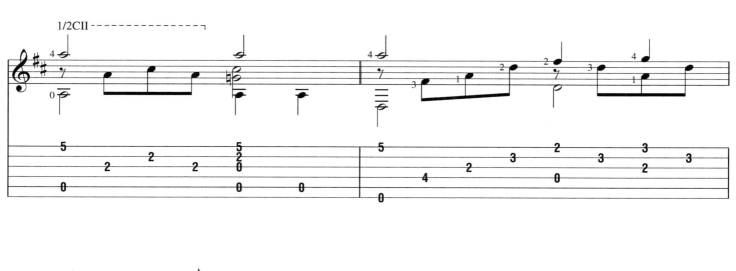

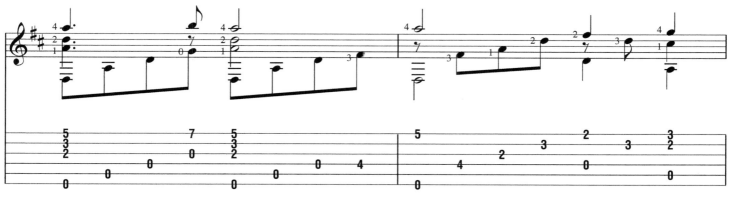

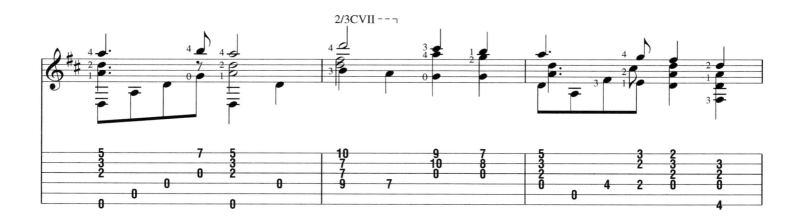

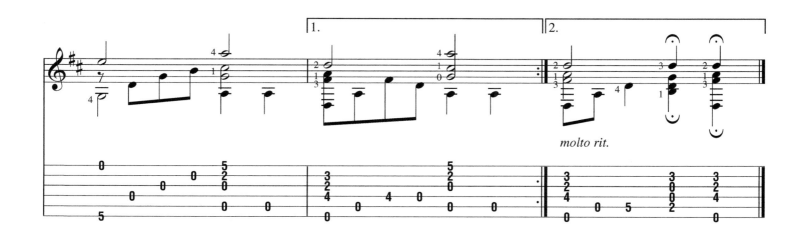

# Nearer, My God, to Thee

**Words by Sarah F. Adams**
**Based on Genesis 28:10-22**
**Music by Lowell Mason**

Tuning:
(low to high) D-A-D-G-B-E

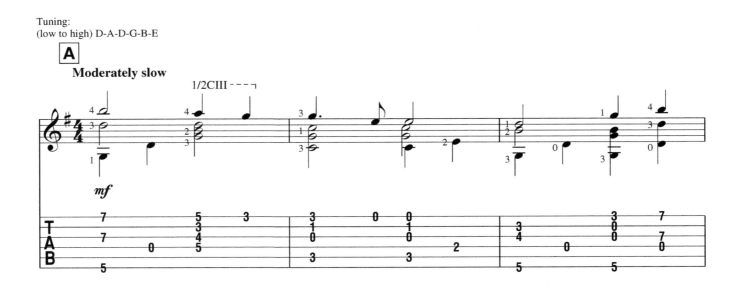

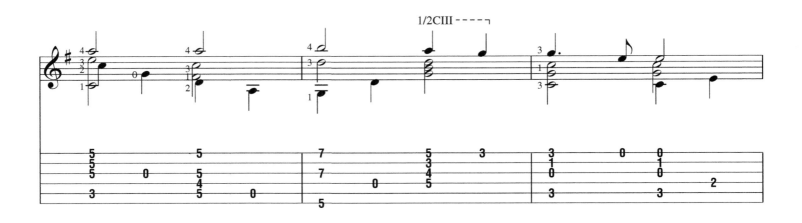

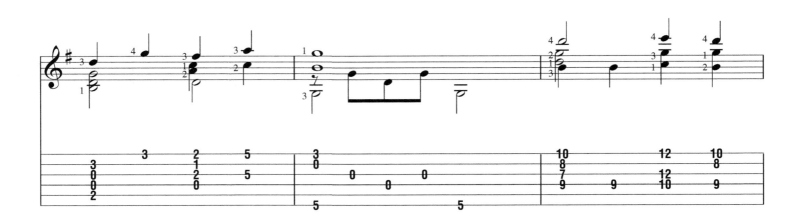

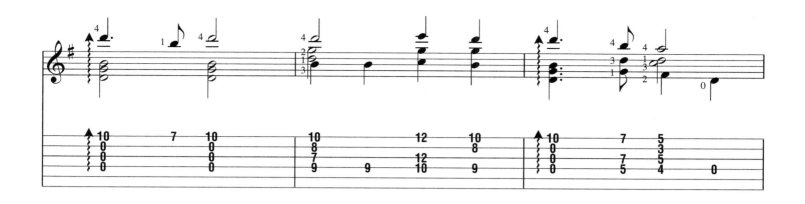

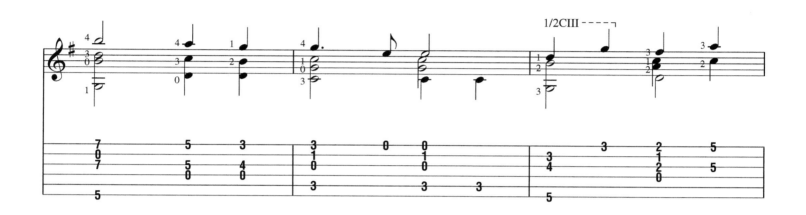

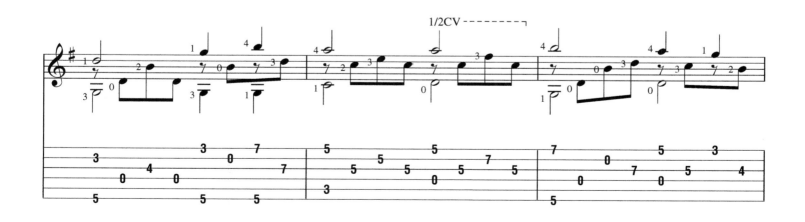

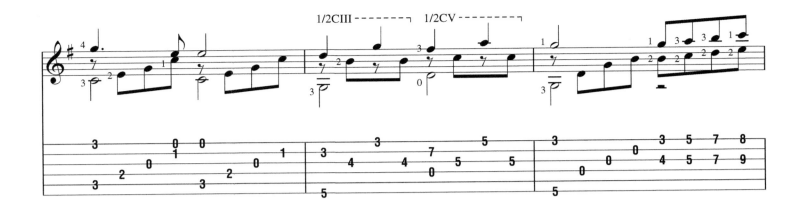

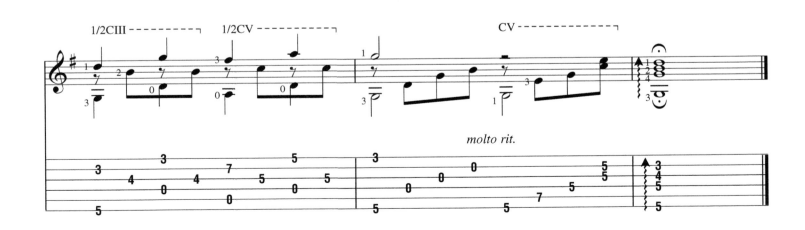

*molto rit.*

# The Old Rugged Cross

Words and Music by Rev. George Bennard

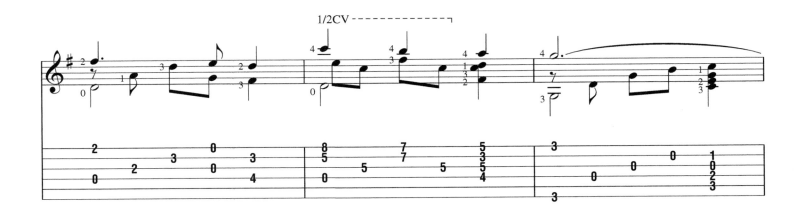

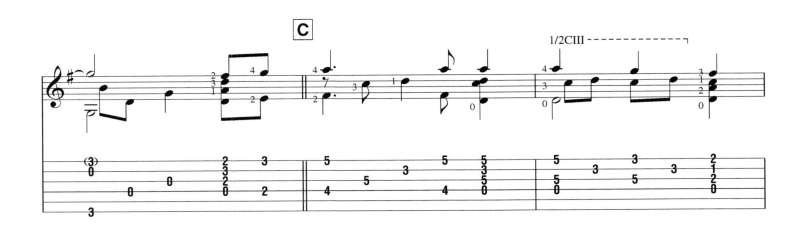

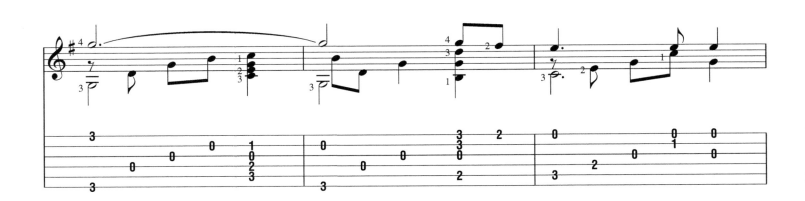

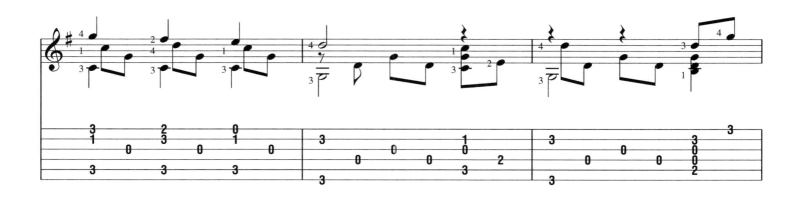

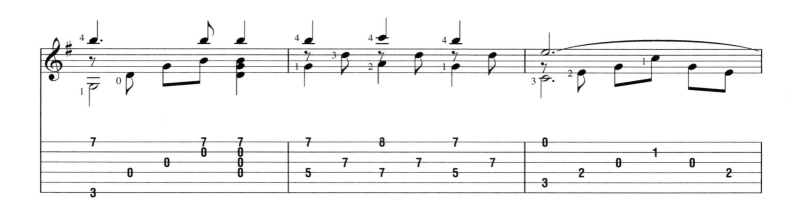

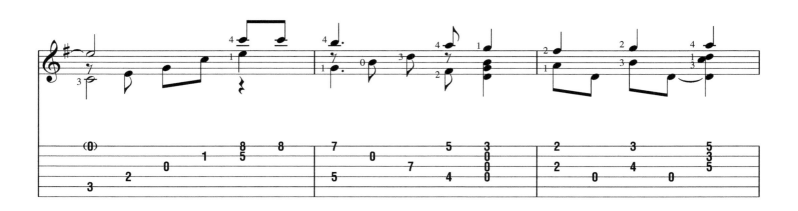

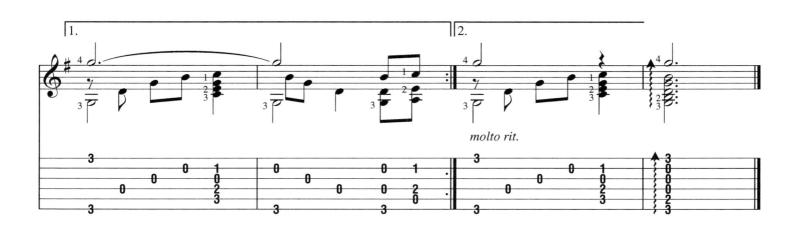

*molto rit.*

# O Sacred Head, Now Wounded

**Words by Bernard Of Clairvaux**
**Music by Hans Leo Hassler**

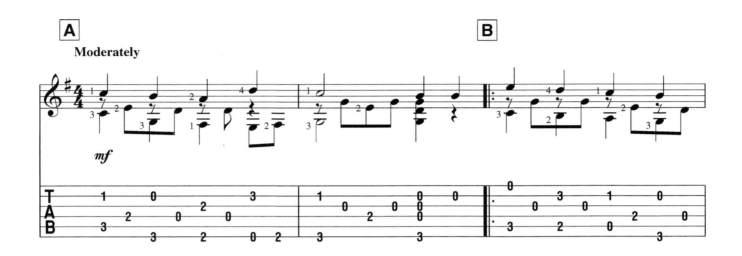

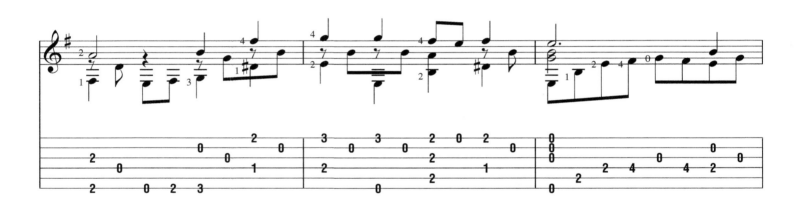

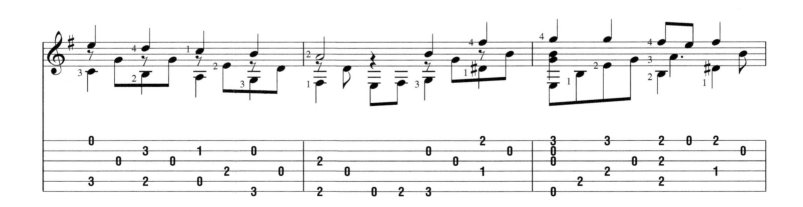

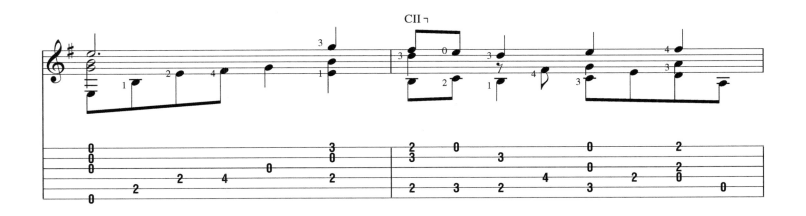

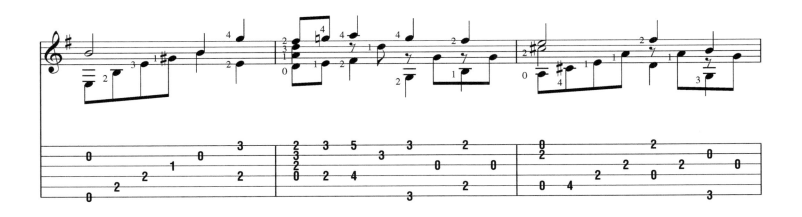

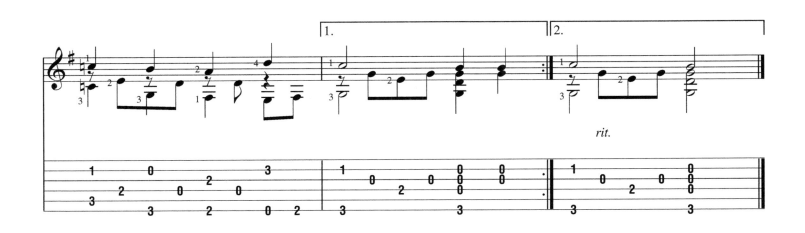

# O Worship the King

**Words by Robert Grant**
**Music attributed to Johann Michael Haydn**
**Arranged by William Gardiner**

Tuning:
(low to high) D-A-D-G-B-E

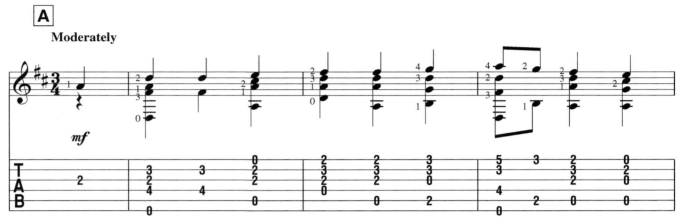

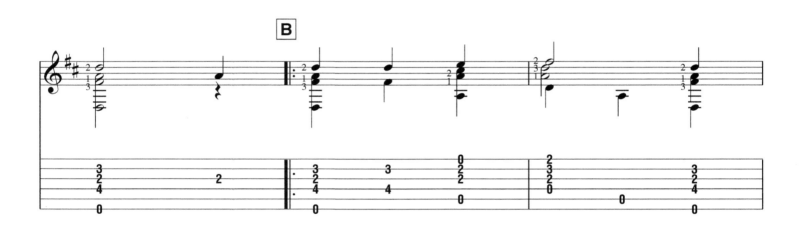

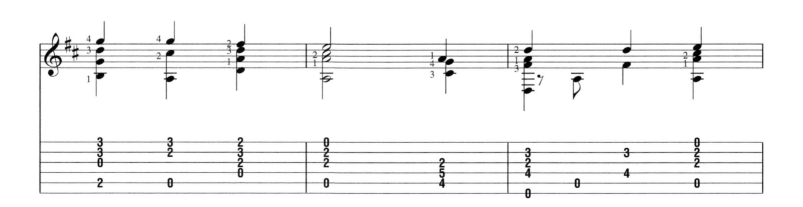

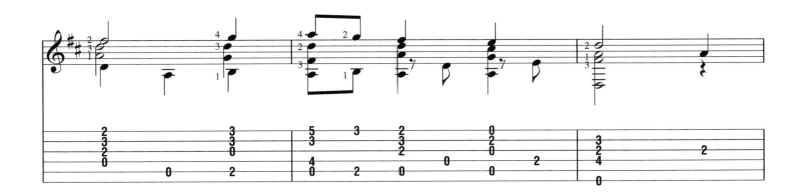

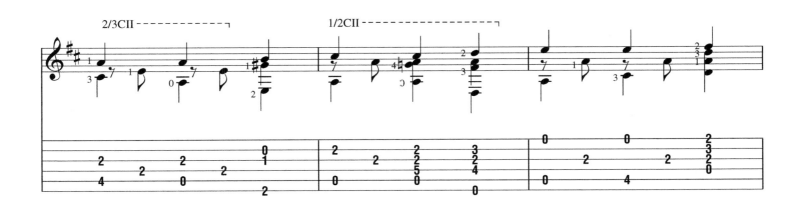

# Praise to the Lord, the Almighty

**Words by Joachim Neander**
**Translated by Catherine Winkworth**
**Music from *Erneuerten Gesangbuch***

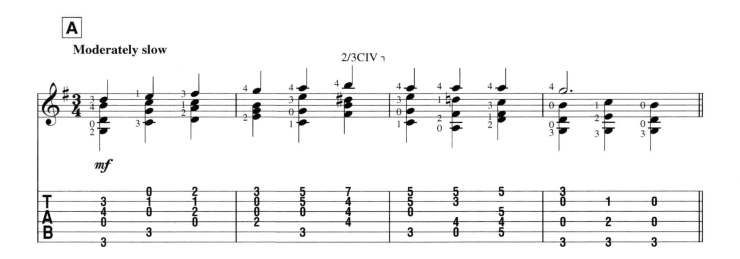

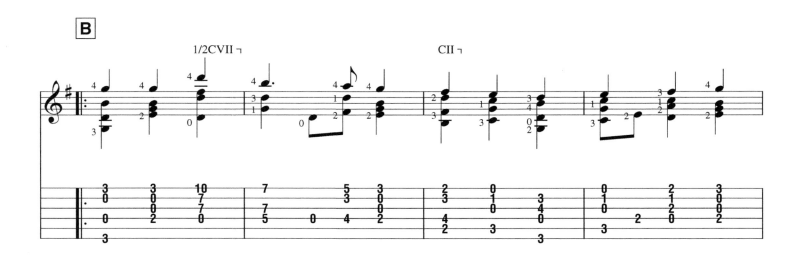

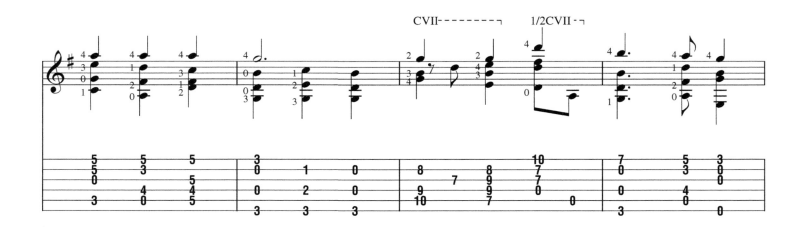

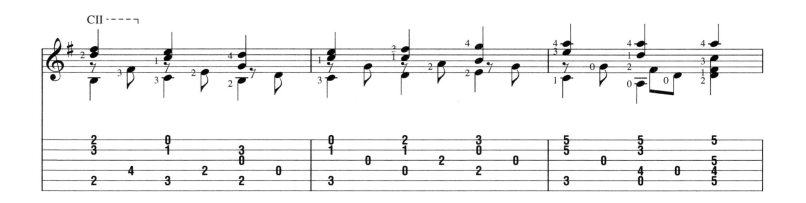

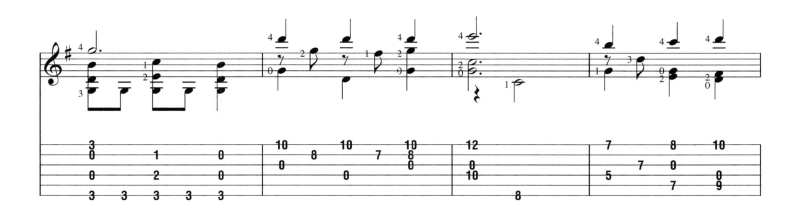

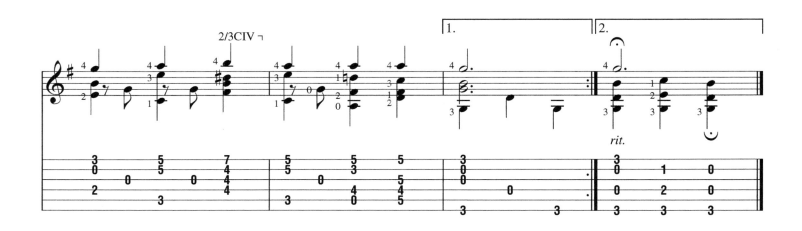

# Rock of Ages

**Words by Augustus M. Toplady**
**V. 1, 2, 4 altered by Thomas Cotterill**
**Music by Thomas Hastings**

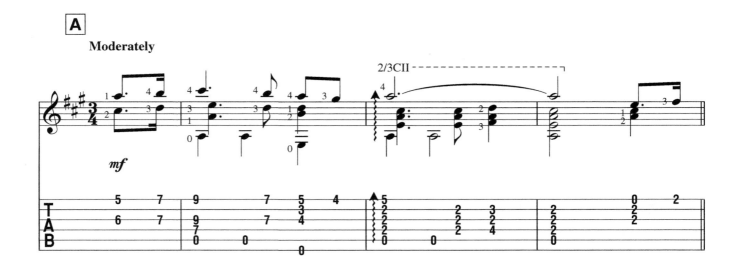

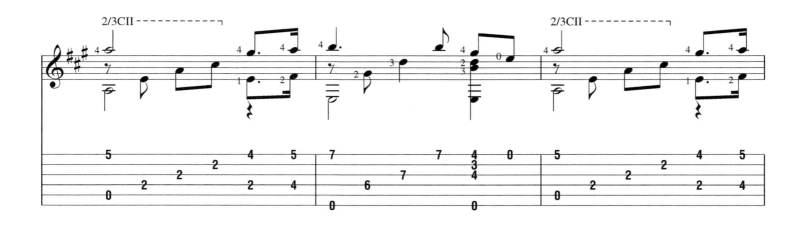

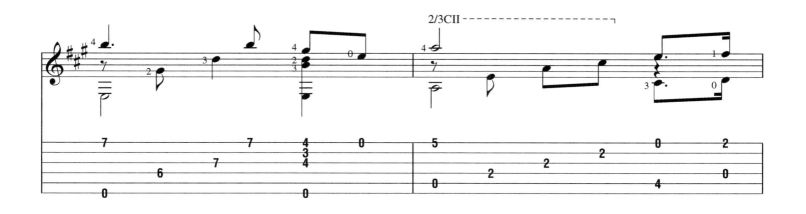

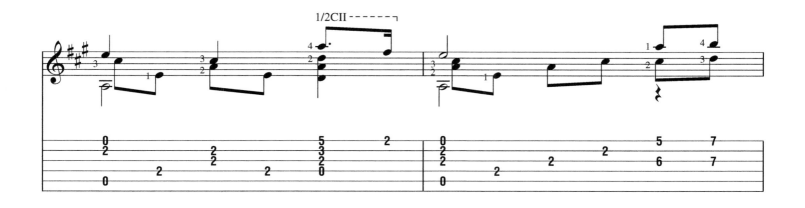

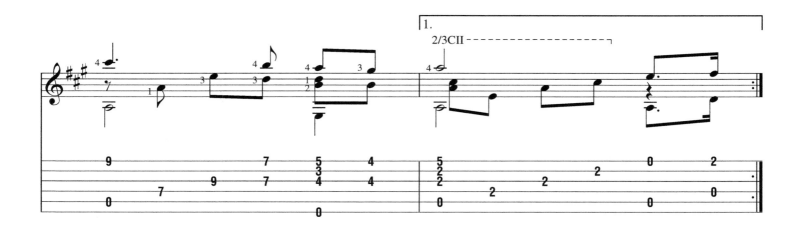

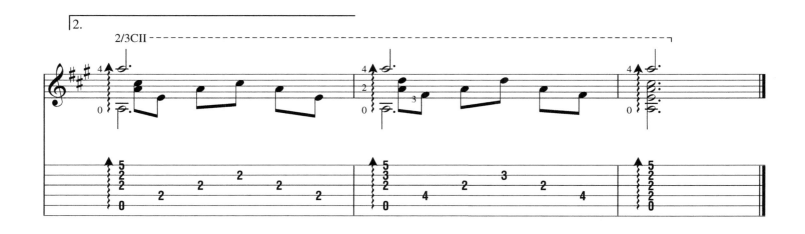

# Savior, Like a Shepherd Lead Us

**Words from *Hymns for the Young***
**Attributed to Dorothy A. Thrupp**
**Music by William B. Bradbury**

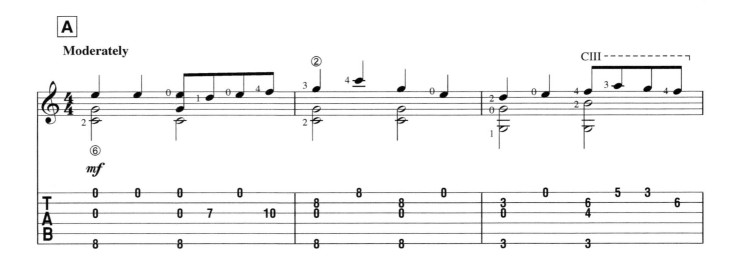

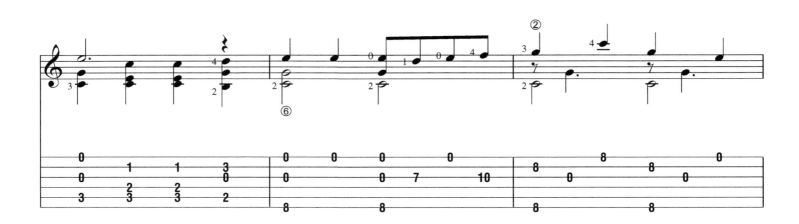

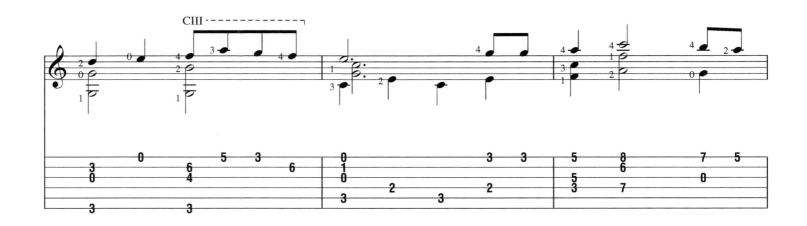

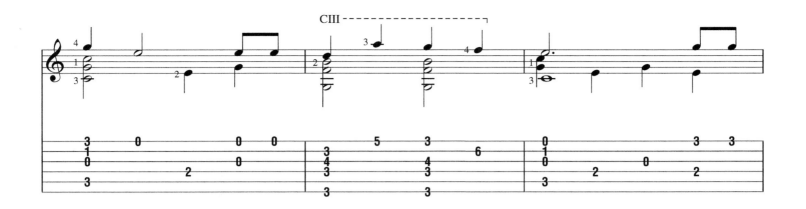

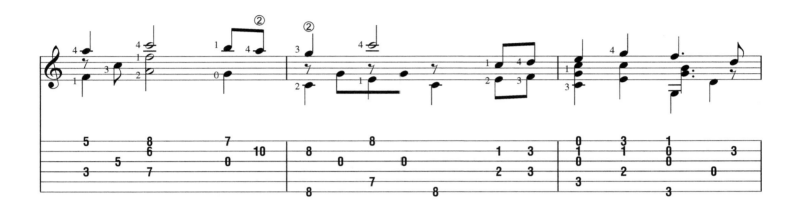

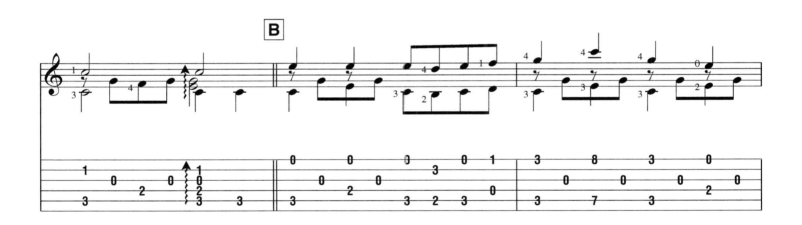

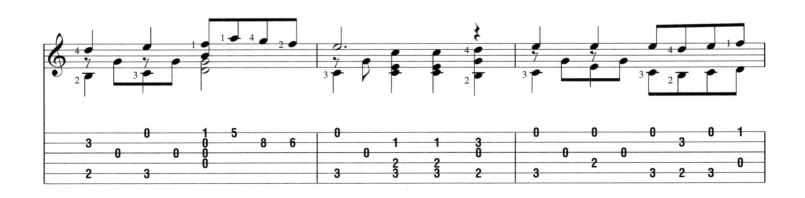

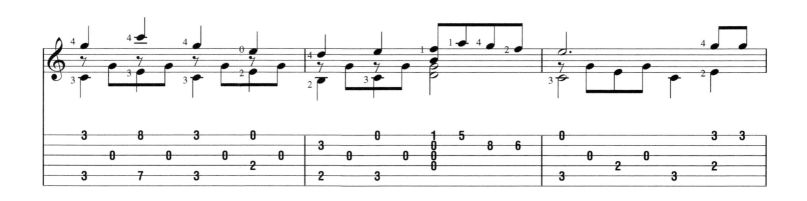

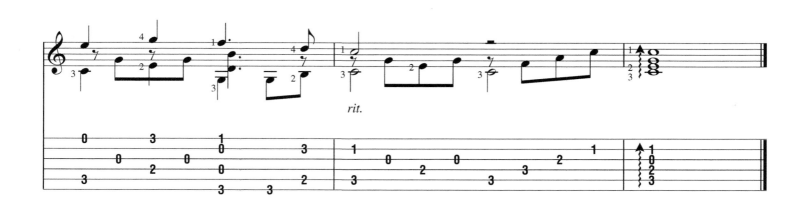

# Take My Life and Let It Be

**Words by Frances R. Havergal**
**Music by Henry A. Cesar Malan**

# What a Friend We Have in Jesus

**Words by Joseph M. Scriven**
**Music by Charles C. Converse**

Tuning:
(low to high) D-A-D-G-B-E

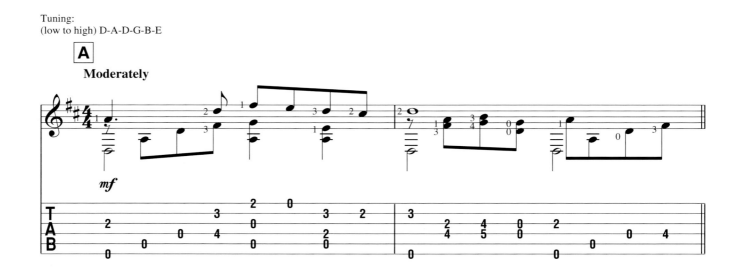

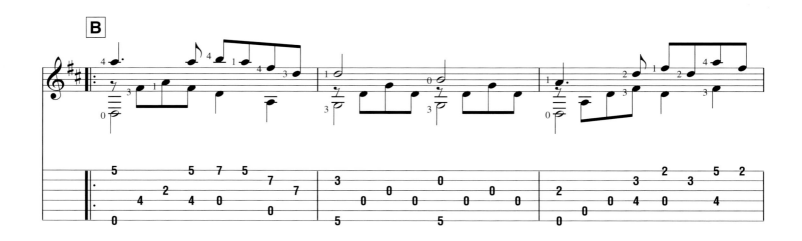

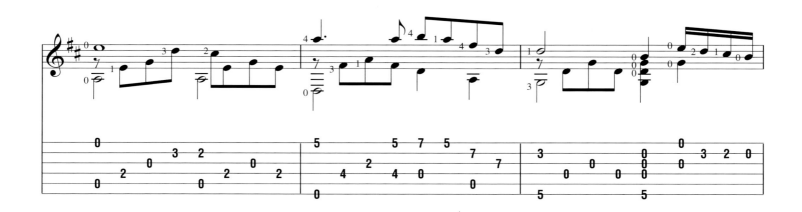

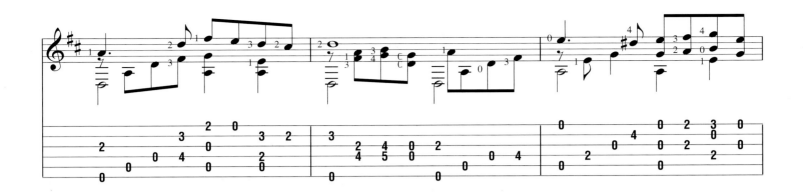

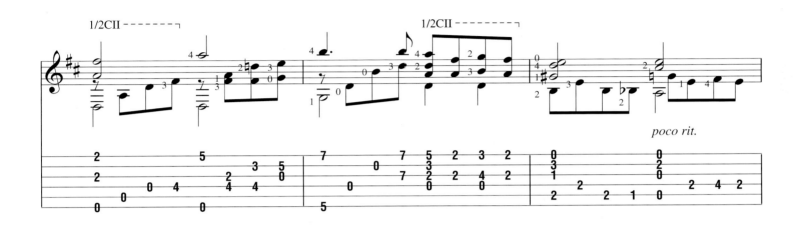

# CLASSICAL GUITAR

## INSTRUCTIONAL BOOKS & METHODS AVAILABLE FROM HAL LEONARD

### CLASSICAL STUDIES FOR PICK-STYLE GUITAR

*by William Leavitt*
*Berklee Press*

This Berklee Workshop, featuring over 20 solos and duets by Bach, Carcassi, Paganini, Sor and other renowned composers, is designed to acquaint intermediate to advanced pick-style guitarists with some of the excellent classical music that is adaptable to pick-style guitar. With study and practice, this workshop will increase a player's knowledge and proficiency on this formidable instrument.
50449440...............................................$14.99

### ÉTUDES SIMPLES FOR GUITAR

*by Leo Brouwer*
*Editions Max Eschig*

This new, completely revised and updated edition includes critical commentary and performance notes. Each study is accompanied by an introduction that illustrates its principal musical features and technical objectives, complete with suggestions and preparatory exercises.
50565810 Book/CD Pack.....................$26.99

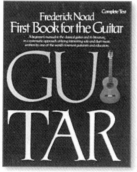

### FIRST BOOK FOR THE GUITAR

*by Frederick Noad*
*G. Schirmer, Inc.*

A beginner's manual to the classical guitar. Uses a systematic approach using the interesting solo and duet music written by Noad, one of the world's foremost guitar educators. No musical knowledge is necessary. Student can progress by simple stages. Many of the exercises are designed for a teacher to play with the students. Will increase student's enthusiasm, therefore increasing the desire to take lessons.
50334370 Part 1 .....................................$12.99
50334520 Part 2 .....................................$18.99
50335160 Part 3 .....................................$16.99
50336760 Complete Edition..................$32.99

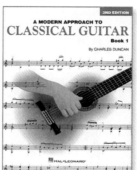

### HAL LEONARD CLASSICAL GUITAR METHOD

**INCLUDES TAB**

*by Paul Henry*

This comprehensive and easy-to-use beginner's guide uses the music of the master composers to teach you the basics of the classical style and technique. Includes pieces by Beethoven, Bach, Mozart, Schumann, Giuliani, Carcassi, Bathioli, Aguado, Tarrega, Purcell, and more. Includes all the basics plus info on PIMA technique, two- and three-part music, time signatures, key signatures, articulation, free stroke, rest stroke, composers, and much more.
00697376 Book/Online Audio (no tab) .................$16.99
00142652 Book/Online Audio (with tab) ..............$17.99

### A MODERN APPROACH TO CLASSICAL GUITAR

*by Charles Duncan*

This multi-volume method was developed to allow students to study the art of classical guitar within a new, more contemporary framework. For private, class or self-instruction.

00695114 Book 1 – Book Only ..............................$8.99
00695113 Book 1 – Book/Online Audio................$12.99
00699204 Book 1 – Repertoire Book Only............$11.99
00699205 Book 1 – Repertoire Book/Online Audio .$16.99
00695116 Book 2 – Book Only ..............................$8.99
00695115 Book 2 – Book/Online Audio................$12.99
00699208 Book 2 – Repertoire .............................$12.99
00699202 Book 3 – Book Only ..............................$9.99
00695117 Book 3 – Book/Online Audio................$14.99
00695119 Composite Book/CD Pack ....................$32.99

### 100 GRADED CLASSICAL GUITAR STUDIES

*Selected and Graded by Frederick Noad*

Frederick Noad has selected 100 studies from the works of three outstanding composers of the classical period: Sor, Giuliani, and Carcassi. All these studies are invaluable for developing both right hand and left hand skills. Students and teachers will find this book invaluable for making technical progress. In addition, they will build a repertoire of some of the most melodious music ever written for the guitar.
14023154........................................................$29.99

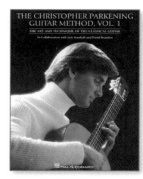

### CHRISTOPHER PARKENING GUITAR METHOD

THE ART & TECHNIQUE OF THE CLASSICAL GUITAR

Guitarists will learn basic classical technique by playing over 50 beautiful classical pieces, 26 exercises and 14 duets, and through numerous photos and illustrations. The method covers: rudiments of classical technique, note reading and music theory, selection and care of guitars, strategies for effective practicing, and much more!
00696023 Book 1/Online Audio ...........................$22.99
00695228 Book 1 (No Audio) ..............................$17.99
00696024 Book 2/Online Audio ...........................$22.99
00695229 Book 2 (No Audio) ..............................$17.99

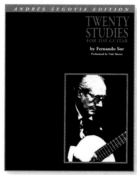

### SOLO GUITAR PLAYING

*by Frederick M. Noad*

*Solo Guitar Playing* can teach even the person with no previous musical training how to progress from simple single-line melodies to mastery of the guitar as a solo instrument. Fully illustrated with diagrams, photographs, and over 200 musical exercises and repertoire selections, these books offer instruction in every phase of classical guitar playing.
14023147 Book 1/Online Audio ...........................$34.99
14023153 Book 1 (Book Only) ...........................$24.99
14023151 Book 2 (Book Only) ...........................$19.99

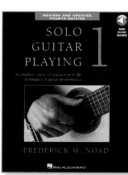

### TWENTY STUDIES FOR THE GUITAR

ANDRÉS SEGOVIA EDITION

*by Fernando Sor*
*Performed by Paul Henry*

20 studies for the classical guitar written by Beethoven's contemporary, Fernando Sor, revised, edited and fingered by the great classical guitarist Andres Segovia. These essential repertoire pieces continue to be used by teachers and students to build solid classical technique. Features 50-minute demonstration audio.
00695012 Book/Online Audio ..............................$22.99
00006363 Book Only.............................................$9.99

## HAL•LEONARD®

Order these and more publications from your favorite music retailer at
**halleonard.com**

0123
005